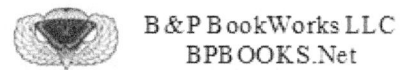 B&P BookWorks LLC
BPBOOKS.Net

TWELVE-STEP WORKBOOK

STEP ONE: Doctor's Opinion and More About Alcoholism

A companion workbook series to Butterflies and Paratroopers Are Not Born with Wings: A Woman Warrior's Guide to Being Happy, Joyous, and Free

MILO

Available on Amazon.com and at BPBOOKS.NET

© 2022 B&P BookWorks, LLC

*Twelve Step Workbook- Big Book Study is a companion workbook series to the main textbook **Butterflies and Paratroopers Are Not Born with Wings: A Woman Warrior's Guide to Being Happy, Joyous, and Free.*** All rights reserved. No part of this book may be reproduced in whole or in part, stored in a retrieval system, or transmitted in any form, or by any means, electronic, mechanical, photocopying, recording, or otherwise, without prior permission of B&P BookWorks, LLC.

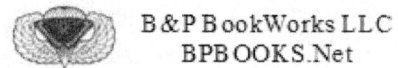

Contents

Big Book Step Study Format 3
Introduction 4
Step One 8
Notes on The Doctor's Opinion 10
More About Alcoholism Thoughts 24
Step One in the Twelve and Twelve 38
Summary 46
Answers 48

Big Book Step Study Format

Step 1, Part 1	Admitted we were powerless	*The Doctor's Opinion*
Step 1, Part 2	Our lives were unmanageable	*More About Alcoholism*
Step 2, Part 1	Came to believe	*We Agnostics*
Step 2, Part 2	Restored to sanity	*There Is a Solution*
Step 3	Made a decision	*How It Works* (p.58-64)
Step 4, Part 1	Resentment Inventory	*How It Works* (p.64-67)
Step 4, Part 2	Fear Inventory	*How It Works* (p.67-68)
Step 4, Part 3	Sex Inventory	*How It Works* (p.68-71)
Step 5	Admitted to God and another	*Into Action* (p.72-75)
Step 6	Were entirely ready	*Into Action* (p.76, paragraph 1)
Step 7	Humbly asked	*Into Action* (p.76, paragraph 2)
Step 8	Made a list	*Into Action* (p.76, paragraph 3)
Step 9	Made amends	*Into Action* (p.76-84)
Step 10	Continued personal inventory	*Into Action* (p. 84-85)
Step 11	Sought through prayer and meditation	*Into Action* (p. 86-88)
Step 12, Part 1	Tried to carry this message	*Working With Others* (p. 89-96)
Step 12, Part 2	Practice these principles	*Working With Others* (p. 96-103)

If you are talking about the problem, you cannot be talking about the solution.

"We of Alcoholic Anonymous are over one-hundred men and women who have removed from a seemingly hopeless condition of mind and body. To show other alcoholics precisely how we have recovered is the main purpose of this book. For them, we hope these pages will prove so convincing that no further authentication will be necessary."–Forward To First Edition (1939)

Big Book Step Study (BBSS) is an approach to working the Twelve Steps as laid out in the Big Book (Alcoholics Anonymous). There are over 100 BBSS Format Groups meeting seven days a week all across the country. BBSS meeting is both live and on zoom. A meeting list, and other information regarding the BBSS format, are available at https://bbstepstudy.org.

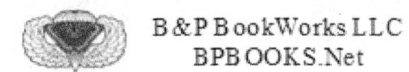

Introduction

The definition of alcoholism is the seemingly hopeless condition of mind and body. The Big Book has two parts; the textbook, and the personal stories. Its first 164 pages are the textbook and include a preface, four forwards, and twelve chapters. The wording of this part of the book has remained essentially unchanged through four editions. As we are on a life-or-death mission, there is a powerful sentiment for keeping the wording as is. This is because what the first one-hundred drunks wrote about us in 1935 still applies to us today. If there ever was a place for the adage if it ain't broke, don't fix it, it would be with this text. After all, if you follow the directions for baking a cake, you will not get a pizza.

If you wish to recover through a Twelve-Step program, we suggest you follow the directions. It is in chapters two through seven, plus *The Doctor's Opinion* of the Big Book, that the directions are codified, or written down as law. Thus, we say if you follow these clear-cut simple directions, not only will you be able to expel the obsession with alcohol, but live a happy, healthy, and whole existence. And while the Twelve and Twelve is a valuable contribution to recovery, its primary purpose is to provide a commentary after doing the steps. It does not contain the directions for doing the steps.

The second part of the Big Book is personal stories. From edition to edition, stories are added, deleted, and shuffled about. In this way, our Big Book acknowledges the diversity of individuality and the ever-changing aspects of our culture. In these tales of trials and tribulation, the miracle of recovery is revealed. And what is that miracle? The problem is removed.

You don't wake up one day and discover you are an alcoholic. You must drink your way into it. This takes time, practice, and commitment. We devote our lives to it. You know what it takes, and you have proved you can do it. So, what does it take to recover from the seemingly hopeless condition of mind and body? It takes time, practice, and commitment.

We often describe AA as "The Fellowship", or "The Program". There is a distinction. The fellowship is the coming together of drunks, winos, alcoholics, lushes, inebriates, bums, and debutantes. The fellowship is our meeting. At which, we establish many lifelong associations, relationships, and friendships. In the meetings, we share our individual stories of experience, strength, and hope in the collective of a society.

1. What is the definition of alcoholism?

2. What are the two parts of the Big Book?

3. Which part of the book has remained unchanged through four editions?

4. True or False? What the first one-hundred drunks wrote about us in 1935 still applies.

5. If you wish to recover using a Twelve-Step program, we suggest you follow _____.

6. In what chapters are the directions codified, or written down as law?

7. True or False? Personal stories are added, deleted, and shuffled about edition to edition.

8. What is the miracle of Alcoholics Anonymous?

9. What does it take to recover from the seemingly hopeless condition of mind and body?

10. True or False? The fellowship and the program are the same?

In short, to save one's self, one must carry the message to other alcoholics that there is hope for the hopeless. Meaning the power of recovery is transferable from one alcoholic to another through identification and strenuous work with each other.

The program is the Twelve Steps. When taken together, the twelve steps provide relief from the bondage of self and take away all of our difficulties. The steps are a program of action, a design for living, and a process of recovery that seems to work with people like us. And who are the people like us? We are the alcoholics of the hopeless variety. For if you are not hopeless, you don't get to a meeting of Alcoholics Anonymous. And if you're hopeless, you may ask, "What do I have to do?"

If you are an alcoholic, you are a sick individual. We know loneliness and looniness, as few do. What AA offers is a way out; one on which we all can agree. For us, there is no middle-of-the-road solution. We have but two alternatives. One is to go on to the bitter end, blotting out of our consciousness intolerable situations. Or two, accept spiritual help. That is what we offer you because it is what worked for us.

Our program of action, though simple, is pretty drastic. It means we must throw several lifelong conceptions out the window. But, for those of us who are utterly hopeless, the moment we decide to go through with the *process,* there is a curious feeling that our alcoholic condition, and not just our drinking problem, is removed. Again and again, this has proven to be. Brevity, clarity, and simplicity is the formula for becoming happy, joyous, and free.

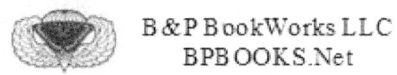

1. To save one's self, one must carry the _____ to other alcoholics.

2. What is the message of Alcoholics Anonymous?

3. The power of recovery is _____.

4. The steps are?
    a. A program of action
    b. A design for living
    c. A process of recovery
    d. All the above

5. The twelve steps provide relief from bondage of self, and _____ _____ _____ _____.

6. Who are the people like us?

7. True or False? There is a middle-of-the-road solution.

8. What are the two alternatives?

9. What is the formula for becoming happy, joyous, and free?

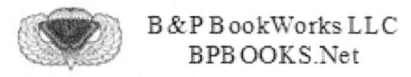

Step One

We admitted we were powerless over alcohol — that our lives had become unmanageable.

Only the first half of the first step has to do with drinking. The remaining eleven-and-a-half steps have to do with getting right with God, getting right with yourself, getting right with those around you, and giving back what's been given to you. Millions have done this. You can too.

The first step has two parts. The first addresses being powerless, and the other unmanageability. Grammatically, what separates the two parts is an en dash. An en dash means refer to the action verb of the first phrase, in this case, admitted.

We find the powerless portion of the step in *The Doctor's Opinion*. The unmanageable part is in chapter three, *More About Alcoholism*. And what do we mean by powerless? Powerless doesn't mean we can't drink, powerless means we will drink. We will unless we avail ourselves of some sort of program of action, a design for living, or a process of recovery. And what makes our life unmanageable? It's thinking that just not drinking solves alcoholism. It doesn't. That's because our alcoholism is with us drunk or sober.

If you hang around AA long enough, you'll see people with five, ten, or even twenty years drink. And they didn't drink because they were thirsty. They drank because their life had become unmanageable sober. The untreated, sober alcoholic, is like that gal in the bar. At meetings, she says, "Hi, my name is Julie. My family is messed up. My boss sucks. And the IRS wants all my money." They think they're sober because they are just not drinking. These are the "half-steppers." They do the first half of step one and the second part of step twelve. "My life's unmanageable. Let me tell you about it."

What these half-steppers are hoping is that there is an easier, softer way. There is not. Physical sobriety does not provide clarity of thought. Elimination of the drinking is but a beginning. To be happy, joyous, and free requires that we used to think one way, and now we think another. For this to happen, you don't just *"do"* the steps; you *"live"* them. This is the principle we must learn how to practice in all our affairs.

If powerless means you will drink, and untreated sobriety means an unmanageable life, why would anyone even want to quit drinking or even try to stay sober? Well, we have an equation for that. It's $(LS)^2$, or Life Sucks Less Sober. If for no other reason, that makes taking advantage of what we offer worth it.

1. What is the first step about?

2. Which part of which step has to do with drinking?

3. What do the remaining steps have to do with?
    a. Getting right with God
    b. Getting right yourself
    c. Getting right with the people around you
    d. None of the above

4. What chapter relates to being powerless over alcohol?

5. What chapter relates to life being unmanageable?

6. True or False? Just quitting drinking is the cure for alcoholism.

7. What two things do "half-steppers" talk about?

8. Elimination of the drinking is but a _____ .

9. What does $(LS)^2$ stand for?

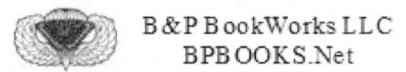

Notes on The Doctor's Opinion

This chapter explains the first half of Step One: We admitted we were powerless over alcohol. The purpose of dividing this step into two chapters is *The Doctor's Opinion* provides the medical view of alcoholism. This is the starting point of understanding we suffer from a threefold disease. One that is spiritual, physical, and mental.

We believe the reader is interested in the medical aspects of alcoholism. William Duncan Silkworth (1873-1951) was the chief psychiatrist at the Towns Hospital in New York City. A hospital with a national reputation for specializing in alcohol and drug addiction. They considered it the Betty Ford Clinic of its time.

The Doctor's Opinion is a non-numbered chapter. That's because it was not in the first printing of the first edition. *The Doctor's Opinion* is about the disease of alcoholism. The doctor writes like a doctor. That's okay. We're alcoholics, not morons. We must become educated on the problem, the solution, and the execution aspects of our mission. The doctor says, "You can rely on anything we say."

In reading the doctor's letters, we see the similarities in the alcoholic's story. However, before any alcoholic will "do as you're told" we must know what's in it for us. The first concept Silkworth stresses are there is no need to beat ourselves up. Yes, we all have a black belt in kicking the shit out of ourselves. However, Silkworth explains alcoholism is not a vice, habit, or lack of character. Instead, it's an illness that associates the extremes of a mental obsession with a physical compulsion, that's followed by the insanity of doing the same thing again and again. This makes those bottles but a symptom of our disease. This means to recover; we must get down to the causes and conditions. Why? Because our alcoholism is an illness where an obsession of the mind condemns the body to drink. And it's the first drink that sets in motion an allergy that condemns one to die or go mad.

Silkworth's contribution to Alcoholics Anonymous was not in what he did, but in what he witnessed. And what he witnessed was the birth of a fellowship where recovery came from one drunk helping another. Silkworth knew firsthand that drunks suffered from a hopeless condition of mind and body. Every day, he saw their self-destruction, and every day he knew he could not help them. He could dry them out, but not get them to where they had any semblance of clarity of thought.

1. The chapter The Doctor's Opinion explains what?

2. *The Doctor's Opinion* provides the _____ _____ of alcoholism.

3. The threefold disease is?

4. William Silkworth was the _____ _____ at the Towns Hospital in New York City.

5. The Town's Hospital had a national reputation for specializing in _____ _____ _____ _____.

6. Silkworth explains alcoholism is not a _____, _____, or lack of character.

7. Bottles but a _____ of our disease.

8. Silkworth's contribution to Alcoholics Anonymous was not in what he did, but in what he _____.

By listening to a doctor who specializes in the treatment of alcoholics, you'll see an essential psychic change, a vital spiritual experience, and the development of a new moral psychology is of paramount importance to your recovery. If you want freedom of the bondage of self, and to have *all* your difficulties removed, then you must understand there is no middle-of-the-road solution.

Physicians today agree with Silkworth's theory that the body of the alcoholic is abnormal as their mind. That those who suffer the alcoholic torture cannot control their drinking because they are maladjusted to life, in full flight from reality, and are outright mental defectives. Thus, any diagnosis which leaves out the spiritual, mental, and physical factors is incomplete.

As early as 1908, Silkworth wrote, "Prescribing practices were doing little or nothing to help the addicted person." After attending thousands of alcoholics, in 1935, he wrote in the Big Book, "We doctors have realized for a long time that some form of moral psychology was of urgent importance to alcoholics, but its application presented difficulties beyond our conception." He said, even with "ultramodern standards," the medical community could not pull the chronic alcoholic back from the gates of insanity or death.

Thus, Silkworth's thinking about how to "cure" alcoholism changed. Instead of focusing on just "drying out" the patient, he encouraged an essential psychic change, meaning something more than self-will, self-reliance, and self-knowledge were required if the individual were to recreate their life.

This revelation was out-of-step with long-established medical and psychological normality regarding addiction to drugs and alcohol. Although he doubted alcoholism was a disease in the medical sense, Silkworth was certain some individuals were "constitutionally susceptible to the sensation caused by alcohol." It was an allergic reaction not found in the average drinker. This, he insisted, made it physically impossible for an alcoholic ever to tolerate alcohol. There is no cure. For these types of alcoholics, their only hope would be total abstinence. And to maintain total abstinence would require a power greater than themselves.

Silkworth realized most medical practitioners were not well-equipped to apply the powers that lie outside synthetic knowledge. To most psychiatrists and physicians, the alcoholic seems doomed. If honest with themselves, they must feel their inadequacy. Although they give all and could offer sound advice, it is not enough. Unable to explain why a change in spiritual psychology worked, when a scientific approach and modern standards did not.

1. An essential psychic change, a vital spiritual experience, and development of a new moral psychology is of _____ _____ to your recovery.

2. If you want freedom of the bondage of self, and to have *all* your difficulties removed, then you must understand there is no_____.

3. Physicians agree that the _____ of the alcoholic is abnormal as their_____.

4. Those who suffer the alcoholic torture are?
    a. Maladjusted to life
    b. In full flight from reality
    c. Are outright mental defectives
    d. All the above

5. True or False? Self-will, self-reliance, and self-knowledge will solve our drinking problem.

6. True or False? Alcoholics have an allergy to alcohol not found in the average drinker.

7. True or False? There is a cure for alcoholism.

8. The only hope for alcoholism is _____ _____.

Though the aggregate of recoveries from psychiatric effort is considerable, physicians admit they make little impression on the problem. Most alcoholics do not respond to ordinary psychological treatment. Something more than human power is needed if an alcoholic is to be brought back from the gates of insanity and death.

Silkworth thought of alcoholics as intelligent, able, and ordinary people in every aspect, except for the effect alcohol has on them. There were the manic-depressive types, the psychopaths, and the emotionally unstable, but most were just "constitutionally incapable" of admitting they were powerless over alcohol. They believed after drying out, they could drink again. This, the doctor knew, was impossible.

As a medical doctor, it was Silkworth who convinced Wilson that alcoholism was a far more complicated condition than a moral failing. Silkworth hypothesized alcoholics have a physical allergy to alcohol, and that the first sip of the first drink produces a "phenomenon of craving." That once they thought of a drink, they drank. And with one, there's always another.

Silkworth made multiple unsuccessful attempts to sober up Bill Wilson. Believing his case hopeless, the doctor told Wilson's wife that death from delirium tremors or commitment to the insane asylum was inevitable. Then, in the course of his fourth treatment, when he was absolutely and positively totally defeated, Bill cried out in desperation to a God he didn't believe in. Suddenly, what he described as a white light enveloped him. This experience is most likely a result of a belladonna hallucination. However, even though he was a lifelong anti-religious agnostic, he still believed there was a purpose, order, and rhythm to the universe. He could accept the idea of a Creative Intelligence, Universal Mind, or Spirit of Nature, but no Czar of the Heavens.

Unsure what had happened, Silkworth advised Bill to hold on to and expand this experience. A great professional risk, Silkworth allowed Wilson to present his conceptions to other alcoholics in Town Hospital. This has become the basis of Alcoholics Anonymous. He pressed upon them to do the same. Soon, Bill and 100 others seemed to be recovered. Where other methods have failed, these individuals accepted the plan of recovery as described in the Big Book.

That no matter how great the want or need, this type of individual could not, not drink. This obsession, compulsion, and insanity seemed incurable. The only possible means of eradication was an entire psychic change. Without one, there is little hope of recovery. But, once a psychic change occurs, the condemned alcoholic could control their need for alcohol, provided they follow clear-cut, simple directions.

1. True or False? Most alcoholics readily respond to ordinary psychological treatment.

2. What brings the alcoholic back from the gates of insanity and death?

3. Silkworth hypothesized the first drink produces a _____ ___ _____.

4. What often happens when alcoholics think of a drink?

5. What usually happens when an alcoholic takes the first drink?

6. True or False? If an alcoholic keeps drinking death from delirium tremens or commitment to the insane asylum is inevitable.

7. True or False? No matter how great they want or need, an untreated alcoholic cannot not drink.

8. True or False? Once a psychic change occurs, the condemned alcoholic can control their need for alcohol.

9. To recover, what must the alcoholic do?

We describe the alcoholic plight as powerless and hopeless. How "not your fault" those two words sound. If this resonates with you, you are at the "want to want to stop" point. You're thinking about who you are, why you are like that, and why it's important to change. Thus, the good doctor's value to AA was not in what he did, but in what he witnessed. And what he witnessed was the birth of a fellowship where one drunk could help another.

Step One says we have an allergy to alcohol; that alcoholism is a disease—albeit a semi-self-inflicted one. Unlike other maladies, recovery comes not only from a change in a physical condition but also requires a rearrangement of thought. As ex-problem drinkers, this makes sense. It explains many things for which we can otherwise not account. This phenomenon is the manifestation of an allergy that differentiates the alcoholic from the nonalcoholic. With the alcohol, no treatment has permanently eradicated allergy. The only relief is entire abstinence.

We believe the manifestation of this allergy results in a phenomenon of craving that never occurs in the average temperature drinker. The first half of Step One does not tell you to stop drinking. Wanting to want to stop drinking is the ante to get into the game. Elimination of our drinking is but the beginning. This means we are powerless over a phenomenon of craving brought about by a hopeless condition of mind and body.

Step One is about the obsession, compulsion, and insanity of alcoholism—not alcohol. Alcohol, by itself, doesn't make you powerless, it gets you drunk. And when drunk, you are powerless over the consequences of drinking. The obsession is when you think of a drink; you have a drink. Then you must have another and another. That's the compulsion. And every time you picked up that first drink, you were sober. That's the insanity. It's our thinking that makes us powerless, and that's the crux of the problem.

Step One is a beginning. There is nothing intellectual about it. Nor is it simply mechanical. There's no direction. However, there is much to learn and a lot to think about. That's why the first step gets two of the seven chapters that contain the step directions. If you're going to do the steps, you better understand what it is you're getting into. You are making a deal with God. And, like jumping from a plane, there's no going back once you leap.

What we offer is of extreme medical importance because of the extraordinary possibilities which may mark a new epic in the annals of alcoholism. These men may have a remedy for thousands of such situations. You can rely absolutely on anything they say about themselves.

1. When at the "want to want to stop" point you begin to think about?
    a. What you are like
    b. Why you are like that
    c. Why it's important to change
    d. All the above

2. True or False? With the alcoholic, any type of treatment will permanently eradicate the allergy.

3. True or False? The only relief is absence.

4. The manifestation of the alcoholic allergy results from what?

5. Step One is about the _____, _____, compulsion, and _____ of alcoholism.

6. True or False? With the alcoholic, any type of treatment will permanently eradicate allergy.

7. True or False? The only relief from problem drinking comes from entire absence.

8. The manifestation of the alcoholic allergy results from what?

9. Step One gets _____ of the seven chapters that contain the directions on how to do the steps.

Alcoholism is with us—drunk or sober. Thus, the conclusion you should draw from Step One is, "The alcoholic, at certain times, has no effective mental defense against the first drink. His defense must come from a Higher Power." Why do we need this Higher Power? Because the obsession, compulsion, and insanity don't go into remission with just not drinking. To overcome obsession, compulsion, and insanity, you must have clarity of thought. And how do you get that? By doing what you're told.

The subject presented in this book is of paramount importance. From its pages comes a program of recovery that has contributed more to the rehabilitation of the chronic alcoholic than all the works before it. It is the basis of an altruistic movement now growing up among them. And while we work out the solution on the spiritual and the altruistic plane, we favor hospitalization for the alcoholic who is very jittery or befogged. A man's brain must be clear of his physical craving for liquor before psychological measures and talk of spiritual remedy will be of benefit.

The unselfishness of these men, the entire absence of a profit motive, and their community spirit, allow them to believe in themselves and still more in a power that pulls chronic alcoholics back from the gates of insanity or death. Approached in this manner, they may be open-minded enough to accept what we offer. Frothy emotional appeal seldom suffices. The message that can interest and hold an alcoholic must have depth and weight and be grounded in a power greater than themselves if they are to re-create their lives.

The leading contributor to this book underwent the "Belladonna Cure". The repeated treatments did nothing to curb his craving for alcohol. It would be "wet brain", the asylum or morgue for sure. Following one such treatment, he experienced a so-called "white light" experience. From which a sense of spirituality, sobriety, sanity, and serenity suddenly washed over him. It catapulted him into a fourth dimension. There was a revolutionary sense of victory. There would be no surrender to asylum, warden, or undertaker.

Bill and these one-hundred others were all in treatment for chronic alcoholism. pathological deterioration, and oncoming insanity. They had lost everything and lived only to drink. They had lost all hope. Following the elimination of alcohol, they accepted the plan of action outlined in this book. From a group of troubling, despairing nervous wrecks emerged, men and women brimming over with self-reliance and contentment. For most, a long time passed with no return to alcohol.

1. Alcoholism is with us, _____ or _____.

2. The alcoholic has no _____ _____ _____ against the first drink.

3. True or False? The obsession, compulsion, and insanity go into remission with just not drinking.

4. True or False? Clarity of thought sobriety comes from just not drinking.

5. AA is what kind of movement?

6. The message that can interest and hold an alcoholic must have _____ and _____ .

7. If an alcoholic is to re-create their lives, they must ground it in a _____ _____ _____ _____.

Wilson, who was more agnostic than atheistic, believed there was a purpose, order, and rhythm to the universe. He could accept the idea of a Creative Intelligence, Universal Mind, or Spirit of Nature, but no Czar of the Heavens. Describing his awakening to Silkworth, the doctor said, "I don't understand and can't explain what happened, but you best hold on to it." It was from this experience he gained some ideas, which he put to practical application. We allowed him to tell the story to other patients.

At age 39, Bill appeared for the fourth time at Town Hospital. He was desperate for salvation and pleaded, "If there is a God, let him show himself?" When the room lit up, Bill, a confirmed agnostic, knew the meaning of spiritual ecstasy.

The importance of Bill's white flash went beyond his personal experience. It validated Carl Jung's belief that something more than human power was needed. That there had to be an essential psychic change, vital spiritual experience, and the development of a new moral psychology. We used to think one way, and now we think another. Bill's initial efforts to sober up the world failed. His preaching was no match for the bottle. Again, following Silkworth's advice, Bill eventually realized there was a distinction between a climatic "spiritual experience" and the educational variety "spiritual awakening." But with both, the essence is a simple belief, God can do for you what you *cannot* do for yourself. On this foundation, he would build a new relationship with God. Here was the answer not to just Bill's drinking problem, but all his problems.

Although sober for the rest of his life, Bill remained plagued with self-pity, resentment, and depression. A drink was never out of the question. He only found relief when working with others. "It's a design for living that works in rough going."

Men and women drink essentially because they like the effect. Even when they know drinking is injurious to them, they cannot tell the truth from the false. Their alcoholic life is their normal life. And unless they can again experience the ease and comfort that comes from drinking, they remain restless, irritable, and discontent. Then they succumb to the desire to drink again. This is the obsession, the compulsion, and the insanity of alcoholism.

The classification of alcoholics is difficult. There are the psychopaths and the emotionally unstable. These manic-depressive types are repeatedly going on the wagon. They are over remorseful, but unwilling to admit they cannot take a drink. After drying out, they think of themselves as cured only to repeat the cycle again and again. Then there are most of us. We are the type entirely normal in every respect except in the effect alcohol has upon them. All of us have something in common. We cannot start drinking without developing a peculiar mental twist.

1. True or False? Agnostic and atheistic alcoholics cannot believe there is a purpose, order, and rhythm to the universe.

2. Bill's white flash experience validated Carl Jung's belief that something more than _____ _____ is needed.

3. The essential psychic change, vital spiritual experience, and development of a new moral psychology mean We used to think _____ _____ and now we _____ _____.

4. True or False? There is no distinction between a climatic "spiritual experience" and the educational variety "spiritual awakening."

5. The essence of a spiritual experience or awakening is a simple belief, God can do for you what you _____ do for yourself.

6. Working with others is a _____ _____ _____ that works in _____ _____.

7. Men and women drink essentially because they like the _____.

8. If you are a real alcoholic, you cannot start drinking without developing the _____.

The obsession is once we think of a drink, we must have a drink. And once we have the first drink, we must have another and another; that's compulsion. And what's the insanity? Every time we picked up the first drink, we are sober. Not once were we drunk when picking up the first drink. This we repeat over and over. We are unaware we must have an essential psychic change, a vital spiritual experience, and develop a new moral psychology if we are to have any chance of recovery. Without which, we remain doomed to face the shame and guilt, and remorse that comes when alcoholic drinks.

Silkworth does not hold that alcoholism is entirely a problem of mental control. Many an alcoholic can go weeks, months, even years without a drink. Then suddenly the thought crosses their mind that one drink cannot hurt them. Having taken that drink, the phenomenon of craving becomes paramount and all other interests are suddenly and inevitably pushed to the side. These men were not drinking out of want. They were drinking to escape the peculiar mental twist that sets in motion the insanity which triggers the obsession which causes the compulsion. Many make the supreme sacrifice rather than fight the obsession, compulsion, and insanity.

What is the solution?

Once the psychic change has occurred, the person who seemed doomed suddenly finds themselves easily able to control their desire for alcohol. The only effort necessary is to follow a few simple rules. Thus, we advise every alcoholic to read the Big Book, and though perhaps at first, they scoff, they remain to pray.

1. The obsession is once we think of a drink, _____ _____ _____ _____ _____.

2. What almost always happens after we take the first drink?

3. What is this effect called?

4. What makes taking the first drink insane?

5. What is required to ensure we have a defense against the obsession, compulsion, and insanity of the first drink?
   a) Essential psychic change
   b) Vital spiritual experience
   c) A new moral psychology
   d) All the above.

6. What feelings inevitably follow the first drink?

7. The peculiar mental twist sets in motion the insanity which triggers the _____ which causes the _____.

8. True or False? Once the psychic change has occurred, the person who seemed doomed suddenly finds themselves easily able to control their desire for alcohol.

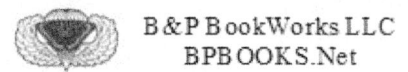

More About Alcoholism Thoughts

Most alcoholics deny they are powerless, hopeless, helpless, and without direction and guidance. Instead, they are constantly asking, "Why does this always happen to me?" "How can I control my drinking?" "Tell me what to do?"

Yet, when informed, that all they need to do, to begin a return to normalcy, is to quit drinking; they balk. Any suggestion they must live without alcohol is not an option. Even when it's obvious that there is a connection between all their trials, tribulations, pandemonium, and predicaments, they cannot tell the truth from the false. Why is this? It's because even the following rehabilitation from the physical, there remains in place the emotional, mental, and spiritual maladies.

Self-will, self-knowledge, and self-reliance always fail us. This is because many suffer from a biochemical genetic predisposition where having one drink causes their ass to stick to a barstool. Then there are those too, who suffer from a grave emotional or mental disorder. Yet, regardless of the primary cause, all alcoholics come with a co-occurring disorder. When they drink, they go crazy. And when not drinking? They go crazy.

With resisting the insanity of taking the first drink, willpower is of no avail. The alcoholics' only hope comes from a change in their thinking, and it is doubtful in most cases even that would have any effect. However, from time to time the alcoholic, in a moment of clarity, understands that to recover from a seemingly hopeless condition of mind and body there must be an essential psychic change, a vital spiritual experience, and the development of a new moral psychology.

Many get to AA because they have nowhere else to go. They have been to detox, and rehab, and tried drying out at home. They've tried inpatient and outpatient. They come and they go. Yet, even though we of AA hide in plain sight, not everyone knows there is a place to go to get a second chance at starting over.

Commitment, voluntary or otherwise, to asylum, hospital, or jail often precedes the discovery of our way of life. We soon know AA is the last house on the block. Thankfully, our primary purpose never lets us lock the door or throw anyone out. If you are even remotely familiar with the consequences of drinking, you are welcome to come along with us.

1. Most alcoholics _____ they are powerless, hopeless, and helpless.

2. What are alcoholics constantly asking?
   a) "Why does this always happen to me?"
   b) "How can I control my drinking?"
   c) "Tell me what to do?"
   d) All the above and more.

3. Why do they ask these types of questions?

4. True or False? We gleefully welcomed any suggestion of living without alcohol.

5. Even when it's obvious that alcohol causes all their trials, tribulations, pandemonium, and predicaments, the alcoholic cannot tell the _____ _____ _____ _____.

6. Why is it an alcoholic cannot tell the truth from the false?

7. Following physical rehabilitation, there remains the _____ _____ _____ maladies.

8. What is the co-occurring disorder all alcoholics come with when they drink?

9. What is the co-occurring all alcoholics come with when they stop drinking?

10. Many get to AA because they have _____ _____ _____ _____.

11. AA's primary purpose never lets us _____ _____ _____ or _____ _____ _____.

We keep it simple; don't drink and you can't get drunk. However, sobriety is more than just not drinking. It's a different way of life, it's a different way of thinking. All it takes is a willingness to learn to listen by listening to learn. We repair complicated people by keeping it simple, and sharing our experience, strength, and hope with each other. Recovery means we used to think one way, and now we think another.

You can't intimidate a drunk. We think we know what we are talking about. We've been there, done that, and got the mugshot. We don't listen; we tell war stories. "Go fuck yourself", our last great act of defiance. That is why the message that can keep and hold an alcoholic must have depth and weight. It is from identifying with each other that we learn from each other. We know how to throw the drowning man a life preserver. Yet, we do not sink the ship to save the man overboard. We help the drowning by keeping our heads above water. This we must learn to do, because our alcoholism is with us, drunk or sober.

Chapter 3 *More About Alcoholism,* refers to the second half of Step One, "Our lives are unmanageable." It says, "… we had to concede to our innermost selves that we were alcoholics." You'll note what separates the two parts of Step One is an em dash. The em dash is not a replacement for "and" or "therefore" or "because." Instead, it directs you to the action verb of the first phrase; admitted. Not only must we admit we are powerless over alcohol, but admit it's the combination of our drinking and our thinking that makes our lives unmanageable. Giving up one without changing the other keeps us emersed in stinkin' thinkin'. And this type of thinking always proceeds with the first drink.

So then, why is it after a period of just not drinking we drink again? It's because we equate just not drinking with sobriety. They are not the same. With sobriety comes clarity of thought. And the clarity of thought comes from being recovered from a hopeless condition of mind and body. You can't have one without the other. That's why it says in the Forward to the First Edition, that we are men and women who have recovered. And recovery means we have transitioned from an unmanageable life, either with or without the drink, into a manageable life.

Step One is about the obsession, compulsion, and insanity of alcoholism—not alcohol. Alcohol, by itself, doesn't make you powerless, it gets you drunk. And when drunk, you are powerless over the consequences of drinking. And it's the consequences that make our lives unmanageable. The obsession is when you think of a drink; you have a drink. Then you must have another and another. That's the compulsion. And every time you picked up that first drink, you were sober. That's the insanity. It's our thinking that makes us powerless to have the power to manage an unmanageable life. No matter how many promises you make to yourself, they will not get you sober. The promises you make to yourself are made to be broken.

1. How does AA keep it simple?

2. True or False? Sobriety is more than just not drinking. It's a different way of life, it's a different way of thinking.

3. We must learn to listen to _____.

4. We repair complicated people by keeping it simple, and sharing our _____, _____, and _____ with each other.

5. True or False? We easily intimidated a drunk.

6. In AA, we do not sink the _____ in order to save the man _____.

7. We help others recover by keeping our own _____ _____ _____.

8. Chapter 3 *More About Alcoholism,* refers to the second half of _____ _____.

9. What separates the two parts of Step One?

10. True or False? The em dash is a replacement for "and" or "therefore" or "because."

11. Alcohol gets you _____.

12. What makes our life unmanageable, drunk, or sober?

Putting down the drink doesn't mean you're sober. Alcoholism is a condition of the mind and body. It's not a temporary disorder. Believing just not drinking is recovery will keep you sober until the day it doesn't. Just not drinking is basic training. When all looks lost without a drink, don't give up, instead give in. Together, you, us, and God bring overwhelming firepower to the fight. Even if defeated the first time out, we can fall back, regroup, reinforce, replenish, and counter-attack. If you've lost your self-confidence and dignity, get it back by fighting for it.

Unlike drinking, which builds us up before breaking us down, AA doesn't break you down to build you back up. Instead, through the repetition of the "Be, Know, Do" method, there is a transformation of thought. It's the same with don't drink, go to meetings, and trust God. We used to think one way and now we think another. We become committed to knowing what to do and doing it. The next right thing is what we challenge you to do.

Alcoholism is with us—drunk or sober. Thus, the conclusion you should draw from Step One is, "The alcoholic, at certain times, has no effective mental defense against the first drink. His defense must come from a Higher Power." Why do we need this Higher Power? Because the obsession, compulsion, and insanity don't go into remission with just not drinking. To overcome obsession, compulsion, and insanity, you must have clarity of thought. And how do you get that? By doing what you're told.

Rehab grads come out all Higher Powered. Being clean for five days (two in jail, three in detox), they are on their way to becoming a YouTube sobriety superstar. "Everything's great; look at me. I'm sober. I've learned my lesson. I've seen the light." Then arises that peculiar mental twist. "One won't hurt. I can control it. This time will be different." They go in and out, roundabout, over and under, but never stop. They either flame out right away or glide along, going down. There must be a better way?

There is. You can join us. However, we can't give you something you don't want. Yes, the First Step says you are powerless, but only over alcohol. It's possible to turn an unmanageable life into a manageable one. It's this new "moral psychology" that is of paramount importance in understanding the full context of Step One. However, without a concerted effort, there is little effect. That's because with alcohol, no matter how long we are sober, there is a drink out there with our name on it.

The ingenuity of AA is drunks stay sober by helping other drunks not to drink. This mutual covering fire provides over-watch when we get pinned down by the trials and tribulations of life.

1. Alcoholism is a condition of _____ and _____.

2. True or False? Alcoholism is a temporary disorder.

3. Believing just not drinking is the same as recovery will keep you sober until the day it _____.

4. AA _____ break you down to build you back up. Instead, through the repetition of the ____, _____, _____ method, there is a transformation of thought.

5. An alcoholic's defense must come from a _____ _____.

6. We need a Higher Power because the _____, _____, and _____ does not go into remission with just not drinking.

7. To overcome the obsession, compulsion, and insanity, you must have _____ ____ _____.

8. How does an alcoholic find clarity of thought in sobriety?
    a) Not drinking
    b) Doing what you're told.
    c) Developing a relationship with God
    d) All the above

9. The ingenuity of AA is drunks stay sober by helping other drunks _____ _____ _____.

Here's our secret: don't drink and you can't get drunk. And the best way to keep a secret is not to keep it to yourself. We tell everyone about it. That way, the secret is safe with us. That sounds a lot like alcoholic thinking, because it is, and it isn't. If you continue using the same plan that has failed so many times before, you must be getting close to wondering what's wrong with your plan. Remember how Dr. Silkworth stressed the solution is outside of synthetic knowledge? Trying to figure this all out is beyond your control. Alone, you don't have the needed power. But when teamed up with us, and a God of your understanding, you do.

The title of Chapter Three is *More About Alcoholism*, not more about our drinking. Why is that? Because our alcoholism is with us drunk or sober. And yet, most of us remain unwilling to admit we are bodily and mentally different from our fellows. That countless attempts to someway control our drinking will succeed is the unrealistic ambition of every abnormal drinker. Many hold on to this faulty belief into oblivion, insanity, or death. Thus, we must fully concede in the first step that we are alcoholics. Going on the next step without this revelation is a death sentence waiting to happen.

And what does that mean? It means when we think of a drink; we have a drink, and once we have the first one, we must have another and another. How many times did you wake up and say, "I will not drink today?" But you always did? How many times did you tell yourself, "I'll just stop for one?" But always stayed for one more. Well, thinking of the drink is the obsession, taking the drink is the compulsion. And the insanity? Every time you picked up that first drink, you were sober. Even when you knew what awaited you, you had no effective mental defense against taking that first drink.

This means we live a life of illusion and delusion. The illusion is the lie we tell ourselves; "I will not drink today" and the delusion is we believe the lie. We cannot realize we have lost the power of choice and the ability to control. If you think that someday you can choose or control your drinking, ask yourself how come you never said no? Remember, it's the lies we tell ourselves that are the hardest to disprove. And even if, by some slim chance, you stop your drinking, the probability is that this experiment will end in relapse. To be followed by even less control and pitiful and incomprehensible demoralization. "We are like men who have lost their legs. We never grow new ones. We get worse, never better." Is there no remedy? Is there no hope? Is there hope of making a normal drinker out of an alcoholic? We think not.

Most are unwilling to admit they have a problem with alcohol. Instead, they characterize and excuse their drinking, saying, "I can control it." "Next time it will be different." "If you had my problems, you'd drink too." Until we fully concede that the problem of alcohol is the underlying cause of most of our problems, we cannot complete the first step in the program of action designed for living and the process of recovery that works with people like us.

1. True or False? Alone, you have the needed power to recover from alcoholism.

2. Why is the chapter *More About Alcoholism*, not only about our drinking?

3. Most alcoholics are unwilling to admit they are _____ and _____ different from our fellows.

4. True or False? Countless vain attempts always lead to some way of controlling our drinking.

5. True or False? We must fully concede in the first step that we are alcoholics.

6. The _____ is the lies we tell ourselves, and the _____ is we believe that lie.

7. A promise that "I will not drink today," but always do, is an example of what?

8. The belief that "I'll just stop for one," but always stayed for one more. is an example of what?

9. Why is it we have no effective mental defense against the first drink?

10. Common excuses for drinking are?
    a) "I can control it."
    b) "Next time it will be different."
    c) "If you had my problems, you'd drink too."
    d) All the above

The delusion and the illusion that somehow, someway, someday, we will control our drinking has to be smashed. No alcoholic ever recovers control of their drinking. This is true because of the peculiar mental twist that precedes the subtle insanity of thinking we can drink like normal people.

As our drinking continues to worsen and the consequences become more severe, we try every imaginable remedy. Sometimes there is a brief recovery. However, what usually follows is even less control. This, in time, leads to pitiful and incomprehensible demoralization. We are in the grip of a progressive illness. We get worse, never better. There is no such thing as making a normal drinker out of an alcoholic.

Most alcoholics, for reasons not understood, will deny, lie, deflect, and deceive themselves into believing they are exceptions to the peculiar mental twist rule and therefore non-alcoholic. For this reason, we pronounce no one to be of our class. They must diagnose themselves. There is no sense telling an alcoholic not to drink because they don't know how to not drink. What we suggest is to step over to the nearest barroom and try some controlled drinking. Try it more than once if need be. It may be worth a severe case of the jitters to understand the hopelessness of their condition.

Does one need to go to AA to stop drinking? No, of course not. There are many ways to quit drinking, but there is no way to control your drinking once you have crossed over into the realm of alcoholism. Maybe, early in our drinking careers, we could have stopped. But during this period, few of us have a desire to stop. And even after stopping, once we start again, we pick up right where we left off. Most of us cannot stop at the first nip of the ringer. We must get pretty badly mangled. This is particularly true of women.

In this chapter, we meet several characters who thought that somehow someway they can control their drinking using self-will, self-reliance, or self-knowledge. We doubt, however, because of the peculiar mental twist, they even want to stop.

A man of thirty was ambitious to succeed. He had seen how his drinking would easily get out of hand once he had the first drink. A remarkable man, he stopped drinking. He would not touch another drop. Self-will would be the answer to his drinking problem. He remained dry until he retired at age fifty-five. Then he fell victim to the belief that his long period of sobriety and strength of will qualified him to drink normally. Out came the carpet slippers and the bottle. In no time, he was in the hospital wondering what had happened?

1. The man of thirty thought _____ _____ could control his drinking.

2. The _____ and the _____ that somehow, someway, someday, we will control our drinking has to be smashed.

3. The reason no alcoholic ever recovers control of their drinking is because of the _____ _____ _____ that precedes the subtle insanity.

4. True or False? Alcoholics someday can drink like normal people.

5. As our drinking continues, the _____ becomes more severe.

6. What do we do to control our drinking?

7. Drinking after stopping leads to _____ _____ _____.

8. Over time, the alcoholic life leads to?
    a. Pitiful and incomprehensible demoralization.
    b. Being in the grip of a progressive illness.
    c. Getting worse, never better.
    d. All the above.

9. True or False? There is no such thing as making a normal drinker out of an alcoholic.

10. Most alcoholics will _____, _____, _____, and _____ themselves into believing they are exceptions to the peculiar mental twist rule and therefore non-alcoholic.

11. There is no sense telling an alcoholic not to drink because they don't know how to _____ _____.

Once again, it's proved, that once an alcoholic, always an alcoholic. Renewing his resolve, he tried every means of treatment that money could buy. Every attempt failed, and he was dead within four years.

If anyone questions their ability to stop drinking, we suggest leaving liquor alone for a year. If you are a real alcoholic, there is a scant chance of success. In most cases, you will be drunk again in short order. We have seen time and time again the promises we make to ourselves are meant to be broken. This is the baffling feature of alcoholism, this utter inability to stay away from it no matter how great the necessity or wish. We describe this as the obsession, the compulsion, and the insanity of alcoholism. When we think of a drink, we must have a drink. And once we have the first one, we must have another and another. And every time we think of a drink, we were sober. That is the mystery of alcoholism.

Our next example is Jim. He had a commendable war record, is a good salesperson, and everybody likes him. He is intelligent and normal in every aspect, except for the effect alcohol has on him. Realizing he would lose everything, he worked with us. He made a good beginning. But failed to enlarge his spiritual life. Self-reliance would save him.

One day Jim went to work feeling a bit irritated. After a few words with the boss, he went to see a prospect. On the way, he stopped at a bar that he was familiar with. He ordered a sandwich and a glass of milk. There was no thought of drinking. Then suddenly the thought crossed his mind that whiskey in his milk could do no harm. He vaguely sensed he was not too smart, but the peculiar mental twist had hold of him. The experiment of putting a whiskey in his milk went so well that he ordered another and then another, and then several more. He had not thought of the consequences, instead, sound reasoning inevitably gave way to some insanely trivial excuse to take the first drink. This behavior is absurd and incomprehensible. It was back at the asylum for Jim. Self-reliance had failed him.

Now about the jay-walker. Many believe this example is ridiculous, but let's look at it from a standpoint of our drinking careers. Here is a chap who gets a thrill out of jaywalking. He knows he is risking injury, ridicule, and death. Even though he knows this behavior is injurious to him, he cannot get the jaywalking idea out of his head. After several close calls, he promises to stop jaywalking for good, but soon, he is back at it. As his conduct continues, he becomes more and more cavalier about his chance of serious injury. He regularly promises to stop, but he can't. Even upon leaving the hospital following serious injuries, the first thing he does is jay-walk again. Such a man, no matter how intelligent they may be in other respects, we would classify this as crazy. Is not this comparable to your drinking?

1. In *More About Alcoholism* a man of thirty proves that once an alcoholic, _____ an alcoholic.

2. True or False? Money can buy sobriety.

3. If anyone questions their ability to stop drinking, we suggest leaving liquor alone for a _____.

4. The promises we make to ourselves about quitting drinking are meant to be _____.

5. This is the baffling feature of alcoholism, this utter _____ to stay away from it no matter how great the necessity or wish.

6. When Jim put whiskey in his milk, he vaguely sensed he was not too _____.

7. Why did Jim put whiskey in his milk?

8. That an alcoholic can put whiskey in their milk without harm is _____ and _____.

9. What failed Jim?

10. What should Jim have done instead?

11. True or False? The jay-walker example exemplifies alcoholic behavior.

Fred is an accountant. He has a good income, a fine home, and a loving family. He makes friends easily. He appears to be a stable and well-balanced individual. We first met Fred in a hospital after a drinking bout where he went to recover from an acute case of the jitters. He was much ashamed of his inability to control his drinking. After speaking with us and learning about what we knew of alcoholism, he said the idea of the first drink made sense. He quit drinking altogether. Self-knowledge would be the answer. Yet Fred would not believe himself to be an alcoholic, nor would accept the spiritual program of action that we offered. We heard no more a Fred for a while.

Here is his story. Fred was out of town on business. Physically, he felt fine. He had no worries and his business came off well. It was the end of a perfect day, with not a cloud on the horizon. In the hotel dining room, he thought a cocktail would be nice. After all, he knew all about alcoholism and thought he was simply making much hard work. One, that would be it, no more. After a couple more, he went for a walk. Why not have a highball before bed? He had one, then another, then plenty more. Fred knows little of where he went and what he did. Not only was he off guard against the peculiar mental twist, but he also made no fight whatever against the first drink. He now remembered what his AA friends had told him. Which was, that if he had an alcoholic mind, there would come a time and a place and he would drink again. It was true; he had an alcoholic mind.

Here is the truth: self-will, self-knowledge, and self-reliance will always fail. We must ground our solution in some form of essential psychic change, vital spiritual experience, and the development of a new moral psychology. The program of action, though simple, is pretty drastic. It means we must throw several lifelong consumptions out the window. But the moment we make up our minds to go through with the *process,* we have a curious feeling that our alcoholic condition, and not just our drinking problem is relieved as it proves to be. The essence of this is the simple belief that God can do for us what we cannot do for ourselves. Once more, the alcoholic has no effective mental defense against the first drink. Their defense must come from a Higher Power.

1. True or False? Having a good income, a fine home, and a loving family ensures immunity from alcoholism.

2. True or False? No alcoholic can ever appear to be a stable and well-balanced individual.

3. In More About Alcoholism, why did Fred go to the hospital?

4. Why didn't Fred equate his jitters with his drinking?

5. What did Fred see as his solution?
6. True or False? The idea of the subtle insanity of the first drink made sense to Fred.

7. What did Fred's AA friends tell him about having an alcoholic mind?

8. Which of the following will work in controlling the obsession, compulsion, and insanity?
    a. Self-will
    b. Self-reliance
    c. Self-knowledge
    d. None of the above

9. True or False? The essence of a spiritual awakening is the simple belief that God can do for us, what we cannot do for ourselves.

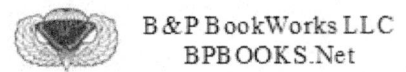

Step One in the Twelve and Twelve

We can sum everything you need to know about being an alcoholic up with two thoughts. First, when drinking, everything falls apart. And when not drinking? Life Sucks Less Sober (LS)².

The basic principles and practices associated with Alcoholics Anonymous are nothing new. Most of what we say about spirituality, sobriety, sanity, and serenity is "borrowed". To prove the point, the fellowship gets its name—Alcoholics Anonymous—from an abbreviated title of the Big Book: *Alcoholics Anonymous: The Story of How Many Thousands of Men and Women Have Recovered from Alcoholism*. You'll note: first, it's recovered, and second, it's alcoholism. One is past tense, and the other is about more than just not drinking.

AA General Services published *Twelve Steps and Twelve Traditions*, twelve years after the Big Book. It's commonly known as the Twelve and Twelve. Its primary author was AA's co-founder, Bill Wilson. The Twelve and Twelve is Wilson's commentary on how Alcoholics Anonymous and the Twelve Steps rescued him, and thousands of other alcoholics from the gates of insanity or death.

However, unlike the Big Book, the Twelve and Twelve is not a textbook. It's a collection of essays that provide "an explicit view of the principles by which A.A. members recover and by which their Society functions." While the Twelve and Twelve is a valuable contribution to the fellowship's extensive library, it does not contain the directions for how *to do* the steps. If you doubt this, consider that in the Twelve and Twelve-Step One gets four pages, while in the Big Book Step One gets two chapters. Don't confuse one book with the other. Remember, you can starve to death reading a cookbook.

Like with the Big Book, there is a strong sentiment not to edit, update, or change the Twelve and Twelve texts. However, in 2021, a few footnotes were added to clarify certain out-of-fashion terms from the thirties and forties. We must counterbalance our mission to be all-inclusive while maintaining our primary purpose to recover and to help others do the same. As previously said, we never lock the door or throw anyone out.

AA is a worldwide fellowship. As of 2022, there are two million people attending meetings in 120,000 groups. During the 2020-2022 pandemic, there was an exponential rise in the numbers.

because of meetings going online. Amazingly, post pandemics, most of these internet-based meetings remain available on aa-intergroup.org/meetings.

1. What thought sums up our drinking careers?

2. What thought sums up not drinking?

3. True or False? The principles and practices associated with Alcoholics Anonymous are nothing new.

4. Where does the fellowship get its name?

5. Who wrote the Twelve *Steps and Twelve Traditions*?

6. True or False? The Twelve and Twelve is where we find the clear-cut simple directions to do the steps.

7. As of 2022, there are _____ _____ people attending meetings in _____ groups.

8. You can find a meeting 24/7 on what AA sponsored website?

No real alcoholic wants to quit drinking; they have to. The consequences of continuing to drink are making their life unmanageable. They are finally face to face with defeat, yet they can't admit they are completely powerless over alcohol. It's as if the long-term effect of their drinking has warped their mind. They cannot tell the truth from the false. Their only hope lies in intervention from Divine Providence. Until we accept this, we will remain doomed to an alcoholic death, insanity, or confinement.

We say AA is the last house on the block. The good news is our door is always open, and we won't throw anyone out. If you have suffered the humiliation of self, and the bankruptcy of spirit, that accompanies uncontrolled drinking, you not only belong but are welcome. In AA, you will find a program of action that seems to work with people like us. And who are people like us? We are the alcoholics of the hopeless variety. For if you are not hopeless, you don't get to a meeting of Alcoholic Anonymous.

However, little long-term effect will come to the alcoholic who shows up but refuses to examine what they are like, why they are like that, and why it's important to change. The solution is more than just not drinking. It's a different way of life, it's a different way of thinking. We used to think one way, and now we think another.

This change is no more evident than in the relationships that develop within our fellowship. We care about each other. And caring about each other is contagious. So, if you have nowhere else to go, why not try on AA and see if it fits? The worst thing that can happen is you see what we offer, actually works. Why is that? It's because that means what we offer is what you need.

Understanding what we get, is only a loan. We must pay it back. We all compulsively need to look good on the outside to hide the storm on the inside. It's one thing to be in the same storm, and quite another not to be in the lifeboat.

When wondering what to do, our brain turns into scrambled eggs with a squirrel on a wheel. Needy, greedy, seedy thoughts prevail. The resistance to change is only trumped by the reluctance to try it. Then, in short order, exposure to those who understand your loneliness and looniness as such few do turns your insanity into sensibility.

1. Real alcoholics only quit drinking because _____ _____ _____.

2. What is it about continuing to drink that makes a life unmanageable?

3. True or False? One of the consequences of long-term drinking is a warped mind.

4. Even in the face of total collapse and despair why can't an alcoholic admit defeat?

5. What must intervene in an alcoholic life to avoid being doomed to an alcoholic death, insanity, or confinement?

6. In AA, you will find a _____ _____ _____ that seems to work with people like us.

7. And who are people like us? We are the alcoholics of the _____ _____ .

8. True or False? To recover from alcoholism takes more than just not drinking.

9. What does an alcoholic need to examine about themselves?
    a) What they are like
    b) Why they are like that
    c) Why it's important to change
    d) All the above

You won't find the word surrender in the first 164 pages of the Big Book. That's fashionable meeting slang we use when we don't know what the solution is. The same is true for gratitude. However, in admitting defeat, one does not surrender. Only that they can't go on. That's why so many of us make the ultimate sacrifice. Instead, we need to give up and give in. Given self-knowledge, self-will, and self-reliance are of no avail in achieving victory over alcohol. We find these "selfies" to be a total liability.

We ask little of you, but we tell you to ask for the impossible. And what is that? That's one alcoholic staying away from one drink, one day at a time. We say the program of action, though simple, is pretty drastic. It means we must throw several lifelong conceptions out the window. But the moment you decide to go through with the process, there is a curious feeling that your alcoholic condition, and not just your drinking, is relieved, as it proves to be.

But isn't it a statistical fact that few alcoholics ever recover on their own? Yes, that is true. You may be one of those that prove this declaration. Ask yourself how many times did you say to yourself I will not drink today, but did? Why is it that if you think you have a choice in the matter you never said no? It's not because you are a failure. It's because there is no middle-of-the-road solution. For with drinking, some people can drink, and some cannot. By now, you know which one you are.

When the Big Book was first published, they directed it at the down and out "last-gaspers". These were the desperate. Those beyond human help. However, once becoming "sold" on the ideas (directions) outlined in the book from which the fellowship gets its name, they got well. This is the how and why of it. Elimination of the drinking is but a beginning. It's the ante to get in the game.

As time passed, more and more became aware there was a remedy for the alcoholic allergy that has plagued humanity since the first crushing of grapes. Such a revelation was most dramatic among those who had not yet hit bottom. Many a real or potential alcoholic, having heard our message, were spared years of literal hell. For them, the bottom had been raised. Not to a point where they could control their drinking, but to where they realized their drinking was much more than a mere habit.

What two words won't find in the first 164 pages of the Big Book.

True or False? Admitting defeat is the same thing as recovery.

True or False? Self-knowledge, self-will, and self-reliance are of no avail in achieving victory over alcohol.

The program of action, though simple, is pretty _____.

We ask little of you, but we tell you to ask for the _____.

We say, the program of action, though simple, _____ _____ _____.

True or False? It's a statistical fact that most alcoholics recover on their own.

True or False? For with drinking, there is no middle-of-the-road solution.

Elimination of the drinking is but a _____. It's the _____ to get in the game.

Yet most of these real or potential alcoholics doubted they would go as far as most of us do. They remained dedicated to the fraudulent belief that one day they could control *and* enjoy their drinking. While this is possible, it's most likely the real or potential alcoholics can only have one or the other, but not both at the same time.

Then, after another series of senseless and avoidable sprees, they are down for the count. Perhaps they say, "Maybe those A.A.'s were right." But, still not convinced, they go out again to try still more controlled drinking. However, once the seed of recovery is planted, it takes root in the mind, and that person never sees drinking in the same way again. Though it may take many years, they return to us again saying, "Tell me what I have to do?" Thus, "John Barleycorn himself had become our best advocate."

Not every AA must hit rock bottom to give up and give in, though most do. They then conclude that powerless doesn't me they can't drink; powerless means they will drink. This makes Step One only the beginning. The remaining eleven steps are there to help us adopt a new attitude and relationship with God, ourselves, and other human beings. However, given that the alcoholic is self-centered in the extreme until they collapse under the lash of alcoholism, do they become open-minded to listen as only the dying can be? Again, we have no effective mental defense against the first drink. Our defense must come from a Higher Power.

1. Most real or potential alcoholics remain dedicated to the belief that one day they could _____ _____ _____ their drinking.

2. While it is possible that the real or potential alcoholic can, in rare cases, actual control *and* enjoy their drinking, they cannot do _____ _____ _____ _____.

3. Once the seed of recovery is planted, it takes root in the _____, and that person never sees their drinking in the _____ _____ _____.

4. Who or what is AAs best advocate?

5. True or False? Not every AA must hit rock bottom to give up and give in, though most do.

6. When an alcoholic shows up to AA, what do they usually say?

7. Step One is only the _____.

8. The remaining eleven steps are there to help us adopt a new attitude and relationship with _____, _____, and other _____ _____.

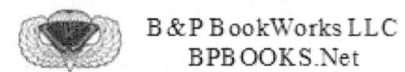

Summary

Until now, I have been addressing the causes of your condition. Which is: when you think of a drink, you have a drink. And once you have the first, then you must have another and another. And every time you picked up the first drink, you were sober. It's the obsession, compulsion, and insanity that make you powerless and unmanageable. You have no effective mental defense against this thinking, which leads to "pitiful and incomprehensible demoralization."

AA says God solves *all* your problems. While it is impossible to eradicate from your consciousness a fleeting thought of a drink, you can learn a new way of dealing with the thought. This requires reprogramming. If you believe, 2+2=5, it's what you think it is, not what it is. Reversing old thinking to regenerate a new attitude and outlook on life requires no longer accepting you are powerless. Instead, you need to be rewired. But without self-discipline, you can't stay still long enough to get the job done. And if you can't be rewired, you cannot change your way of thinking. So, the first takeaway of the first step is being reprogrammed to believe Life Sucks Less Sober $(LS)^2$.

Powerless and unmanageability don't mean you can't drink. It means you will drink. You will unless you come to believe in a Power greater than yourself. If you're reading this, you're likely aware AA is a spiritual program of action. AA is not a religion, it's a set of principles, spiritual in nature, that if followed, will not only expel the obsession for alcohol, but allow the practitioner to live a happy, healthy, and whole existence, no matter what their present circumstances. Or, as cited in the reading, following the directions is a form of 'self-insurance' that yields to a restoration of physical, mental, and spiritual health.

For those who do become sold on the ideas in the Big Book, there is hope. And from that hope, there comes an awareness that God can do for them, what they cannot do for themselves.

And thus, we grow, and so can you. Though you be but one person with our book in your hand, we believe, and hope, it contains all you need to begin. To duplicate what we have accomplished is simply a matter of willingness, patience, and labor.

1. What are the causes and conditions of your alcoholism?
    a) When you think of a drink, you have a drink
    b) Once you have the first, then you must have another and another.
    c) Every time you picked up the first drink, you were sober.
    d) All the above

2. Thinking of a drink is the _____.

3. The first drink sets in motion the _____.

4. What condition precedes the thought of the first drink? _____.

5. The first take-away of the first step is _____ _____ _____ _____ $(LS)^2$.

6. True or False? AA is a religious cult.

7. Following the directions is a form of 'self-insurance' which yields to a restoration of _____, _____, and _____.

Answers

Answers page 5

1. A hopeless condition of mind and body
2. Textbook and personal stories
3. The first 164 pages
4. True
5. The directions
6. Charters 2-7, plus Doctor's Opinion
7. True
8. The problem has been removed
9. Time, practice, and commitment
10. False

Answers page 7

1. Message
2. There is hope for the hopeless
3. Transferable
4. All the above
5. Take away all our difficulties
6. We are alcoholics of the hopeless variety
7. False
8. Go on to the bitter end or accept spiritual help
9. Brevity, clarity, simplicity

Answers page 9

1. Powerlessness and unmanageability
2. The first half of the first step
3. None of the above
4. The Doctor's Opinion
5. More about Alcoholism
6. False
7. May life is unmanageable. Let me tell you about it.
8. Beginning
9. Life Sucks Less Sober

Answers page 11

1. The first half of the first step
2. Medical view
3. Spiritual, physical, and mental
4. Chief psychiatrist
5. Alcohol and drug addiction
6. Vice, habit
7. Symptom
8. Witnessed

Answers page 13

1. Paramount importance
2. Middle-of-the-road solution
3. Body, mind
4. All the above
5. False
6. False
7. False
8. Total abstinence

Answers page 15

1. False
2. Something more than human power
3. Phenomenon of craving
4. They drink
5. They have another
6. True
7. True
8. True
9. Follow clear-cut, simple directions

Answers page 17

1. All the above
2. False
3. False
4. Phenomenon of craving
5. Obsession, compulsion, insanity
6. All the above
7. False
8. False
9. Phenomenon of craving
10. Two

Answers page 19

1. Drunk or sober
2. Effective mental defense
3. False
4. False
5. Altruistic
6. Depth and weight

7. Power greater than themselves

Answers page 21

1. False
2. Human power
3. One way, think another
4. False
5. Cannot
6. Design for living, rough going
7. Effect
8. Peculiar mental twist

Answers page 23

1. We must have a drink
2. We have another and another
3. Compulsion
4. We were sober
5. All the above
6. Shame, guilt and remorse
7. Obsession, compulsion
8. True

Answers page 25

1. Deny
2. All the above
3. They are without direction and guidance
4. False
5. True from the false
6. We lie to ourselves
7. Emotional, mental, and spiritual
8. They go crazy
9. They go crazy
10. Nowhere else to go
11. Lock the door or throw anyone out

Answers page 27

1. Don't drink and you can't get drunk
2. True
3. Learn
4. Experience, strength, and hope
5. False
6. Ship, overboard
7. Head above water
8. Step one
9. An em-dash
10. False
11. Drunk

12. The consequences of our actions

Answers page 29

1. Mind and body
2. False
3. Doesn't, Be Know Do
4. Higher power
5. Obsession, compulsion, and insanity
6. Clarity of thought
7. All the above
8. Not to drink

Answers page 31

1. False
2. Because our alcoholism is with us drunk or sober
3. Bodily and mentally
4. False
5. True
6. Illusion, delusion
7. The illusion
8. The delusion
9. We believe the lies we tell ourselves
10. All the above

Answers page 33

1. Self-will
2. Delusion and the delusion
3. Peculiar mental twist
4. False
5. Consequences
6. Every imaginable remedy
7. Even less control
8. All the above
9. True
10. Lie, deflect, and deceive
11. Not drink

Answers page 35

1. Always
2. False
3. Year
4. Broken
5. Inability
6. Smart
7. He thought he could do no harm
8. Absurd and incomprehensible
9. Self-reliance

10. Enlarge his spiritual life
11. True

8. True
9. All the above

Answers page 37

1. False
2. False
3. Cure a case of the jitters
4. He didn't believe he was an alcoholic
5. Self-knowledge
6. True
7. He would drink again
8. None of the above
9. True

Answers page 39

1. Everything falls apart
2. Life Sucks Less Sober (LS)²
3. True
4. The title of the Big Book
5. Bill Wilson
6. False
7. Two million. 120,000
8. aa-intergroup.org/meetings

Answers page 41

1. They have to
2. The consequences
3. True
4. They can't tell the true from the false
5. Divine Providence
6. Program of action
7. Hopeless variety

Answers page 43

1. Surrender and gratitude
2. False
3. True
4. Drastic
5. Impossible
6. Is pretty drastic
7. False
8. True
9. Beginning, ante

Answers page 45

1. Control *and* enjoy
2. Both at the same time
3. Same way again
4. John Barleycorn
5. True
6. What do I have to do?
7. Beginning
8. God, ourselves, and other human beings

Answers page 47

1. All the above
2. Obsession
3. Compulsion
4. Insanity
5. Life Sucks Less Sober
6. False
7. Physical, mental, and spiritual health

Printed in Great Britain
by Amazon